The Boy and the Eagle
A Pima Folk Tale

retold by Christopher Keane

illustrated by Donna Perrone

MODERN CURRICULUM PRESS

Pearson Learning Group

In the shadow of a black mountain, near a desert stream, there once lived a Pima boy named Kelihi. As the oldest of five brothers and sisters, Kelihi had many chores. Too many, he sometimes thought!

He was responsible for helping his father grow cotton and corn. Beans and squash also needed his care. And in the desert, he hunted rabbits, quail, and lizards.

There was much to do every day, but twelve-year-old Kelihi wished for something more. He wished for adventure.

One day, while he was working in the field, a shadow passed over him. He looked up and saw an eagle. The eagle glided over the desert and sailed above the mountain. Kelihi imagined spreading his own wings and soaring above the cliffs. He wondered what it was like high on the mountain. Then he thought about the eagle's nest. He knew it was a great thing to find an eagle's nest.

"Father, I want to climb the mountain and look for an eagle's nest," he said.

"That isn't easy," his father said. "The mountain is a hard obstacle to climb. And you have to be lucky enough to find a nest."

"But *you* did it," said Kelihi.

His father smiled. "Yes, but I went with my father, who taught me much about the eagle. That is our tradition. Someday, when you are older, I will go with you too."

"I'll be older tomorrow," said Kelihi.

His father laughed. "Not tomorrow. It's harvest time. I need your help with the beans and the corn."

Kelihi stomped away, disappointed.

"Beans and corn," grumbled Kelihi. "Eagles are more meaningful—much more important than beans and corn! Why must I wait?"

Kelihi decided not to wait.

The next morning, Kelihi awoke before dawn. He moved quietly so that he would not wake his family. He packed cornbread and dried meat into a leather pouch. He filled a gourd with cool water and then slung the hollowed-out squash over his back. Then he left, leaving his family sleeping in the ramada, the open structure close to the house. Finally he headed toward the mountain.

Kelihi walked for many hours. Rabbits scurried among the cactus. Lizards darted up the mesquite trees. At last, he came to the foot of the mountain. Looking up, he saw the high cliffs where the eagles lived. Slowly Kelihi began to climb.

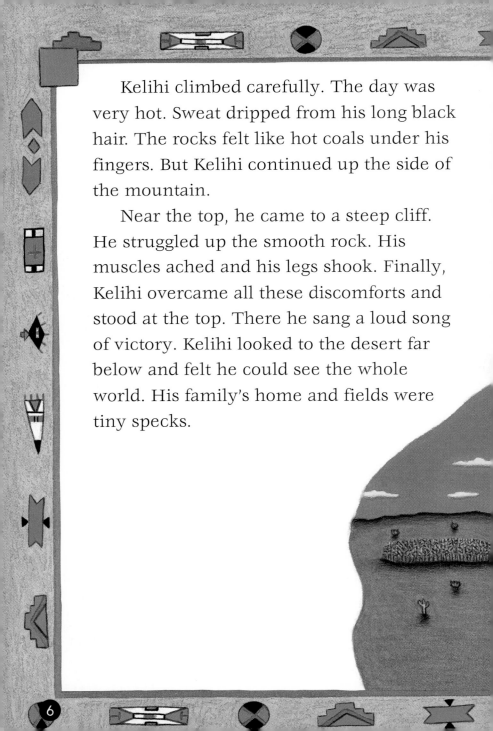

Kelihi climbed carefully. The day was very hot. Sweat dripped from his long black hair. The rocks felt like hot coals under his fingers. But Kelihi continued up the side of the mountain.

Near the top, he came to a steep cliff. He struggled up the smooth rock. His muscles ached and his legs shook. Finally, Kelihi overcame all these discomforts and stood at the top. There he sang a loud song of victory. Kelihi looked to the desert far below and felt he could see the whole world. His family's home and fields were tiny specks.

Kelihi searched the mountaintop. He searched trees, caves, and crevices, or cracks in the rock. Soon, he heard chirping and followed the sound. On a small ledge above a cliff was an eagle's nest. The chirping came from inside the nest.

Kelihi climbed to the ledge. Balancing on the edge, he looked into the nest and saw two baby eagles. Soft downy feathers covered their bodies. The two small eagles looked like fluffy little storm clouds—with tiny eyes.

The small birds shrieked at Kelihi as their mouths gaped with hunger.

Kelihi opened his pouch. He tore off bits of the dried meat and dropped them into the birds' mouths. The eaglets gulped the food and then cried for more.

Kelihi laughed to see the birds eat. He was happy, knowing he had found an eagle's nest. It was a great day.

Then he felt anxious as he began to think about his father. "I hope he will forgive me," Kelihi said aloud.

Then Kelihi looked back at the eaglets and longed to feel the downy feathers. So he reached for the closest bird. But *snap!* It pecked at his fingers. Startled, Kelihi slipped backward. Then in a flash, he fell from the ledge.

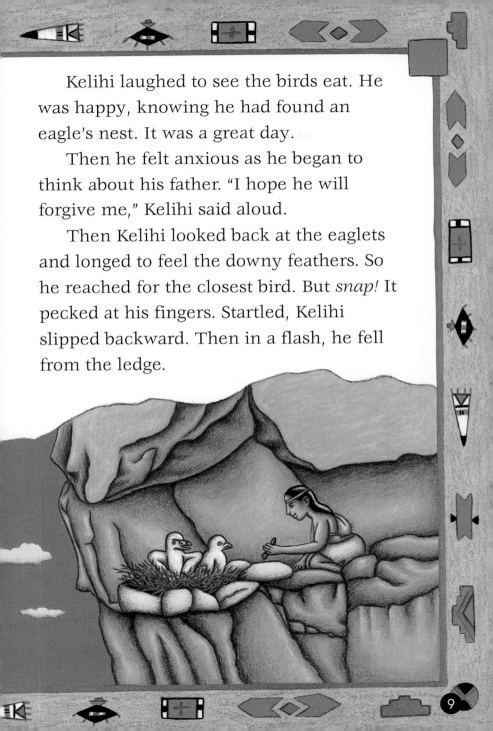

Kelihi tumbled down the cliff. He bounced over rocks. He fell through thorn bushes. Finally, he landed on a small ledge in the middle of a sheer cliff.

His hands were bruised. His knees were scraped. When he tried to rise, he found that his right ankle was too weak to support him. Kelihi knew he could climb no further. He sat on the ledge and looked all around. There was no way up and there was no way down.

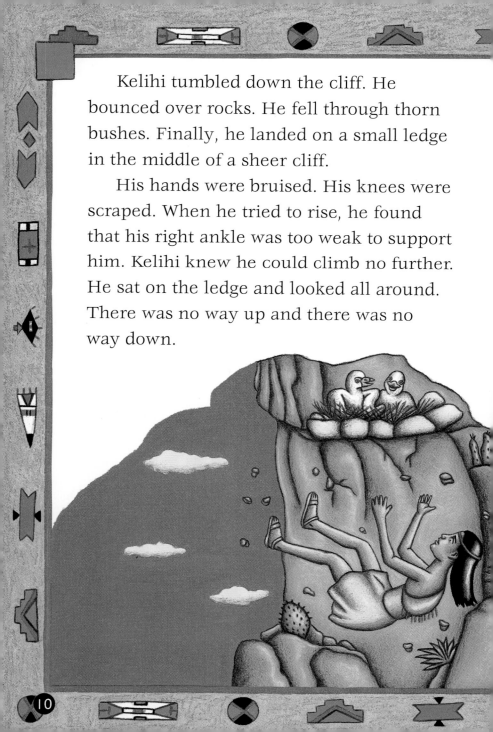

Kelihi began to sob. "Why didn't I obey Father? Why did I sneak away?" he said. Now Kelihi was regretting his entire adventure on the mountain.

Then he caught his breath and tried to think of what his father might do if he were there.

"When you are in trouble," his father always said, "it is best to try to relax, stand back, and look at the problem. Then you will see things more clearly."

So Kelihi tried to relax and see things more clearly. He lay back on the smooth rock and closed his eyes. After a while, he fell asleep.

Kelihi dreamed of a huge eagle. The eagle glided down and landed beside him. It cocked its great head toward him and began to speak. Kelihi was startled when the eagle said his name.

"Kelihi, don't be surprised. In dreams, all animals speak," said the gigantic eagle.

The eagle continued, "I was watching you. The baby eagles are my children. I am responsible for their safety. I could never let you touch them."

"I'm sorry," answered Kelihi. "I never meant to harm them."

Then Kelihi promised he would respect the eaglets and he would never try to touch them again.

The eagle looked hard at Kelihi, and then told him to climb on its back. Kelihi pulled his bruised body onto the mighty bird. The feathers felt warm and tickled his skin. The eagle, spreading its wings and without looking back, soared off the ledge.

Kelihi gasped as the eagle swooped down. The wind breezed against his face as the eagle flew in huge circles. It flew past the cliffs and sailed over mountain streams. Then, gently, it landed in the desert near a prickly pear cactus. Amazed, Kelihi slid off the eagle's back. He sang his thanks and the great bird flew away.

Suddenly Kelihi woke up. He was still lying on his back and sighed when he realized he had only been dreaming. But when he sat up, he saw he was no longer on the mountain. He was in the desert, near his family's home.

Then he looked on the ground beside him and saw a tail feather of the great eagle. At that moment, Kelihi knew that his time with the eagle was not a dream. Only with the eagle's help could he have survived his fall and ended up near home.

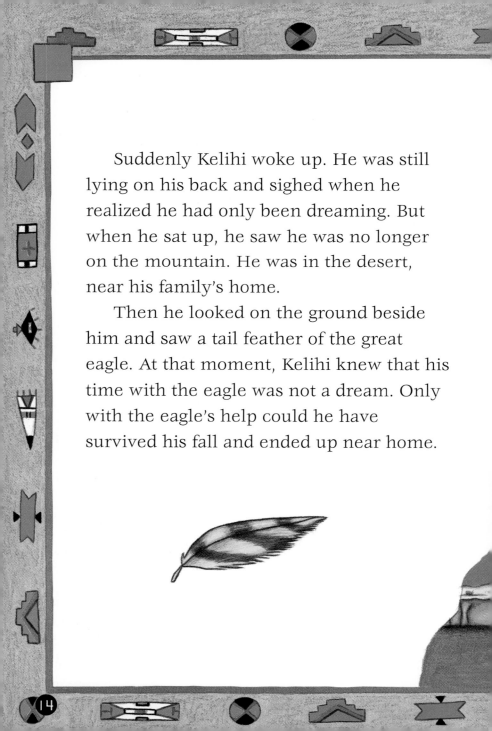

As Kelihi walked home, he realized his body was healed. Not even his ankle hurt. When his worried mother and father saw him, they rushed to hug him. Then they scolded him for running off to find the eagle by himself.

"I'm so sorry," Kelihi moaned. "It was wrong not to obey you, Father. From now on, I will listen to you and I will have patience."

Then he pulled the giant eagle feather from his pouch and held it up in the gentle breeze.

His father looked at the feather and said, "There must, indeed, be a story to go with this feather. I can only imagine what you overcame to find it and bring it home. One thing I'm sure of is that now you understand more about the greatness of the eagle. And the importance of our traditions."

Kelihi looked at his father's strong, loving face. Then he took his father's hand and placed the great feather lightly on the open palm.